Trekking Downrange

Trekking Downrange

Poems by

James Allen Breitweser

Cover design by Shay Culligan
Author photo by Nathalie Walker

ISBN: 978-1-63980-385-9

Kelsay Books
502 South 1040 East, A-119
American Fork, Utah 84003
Kelsaybooks.com

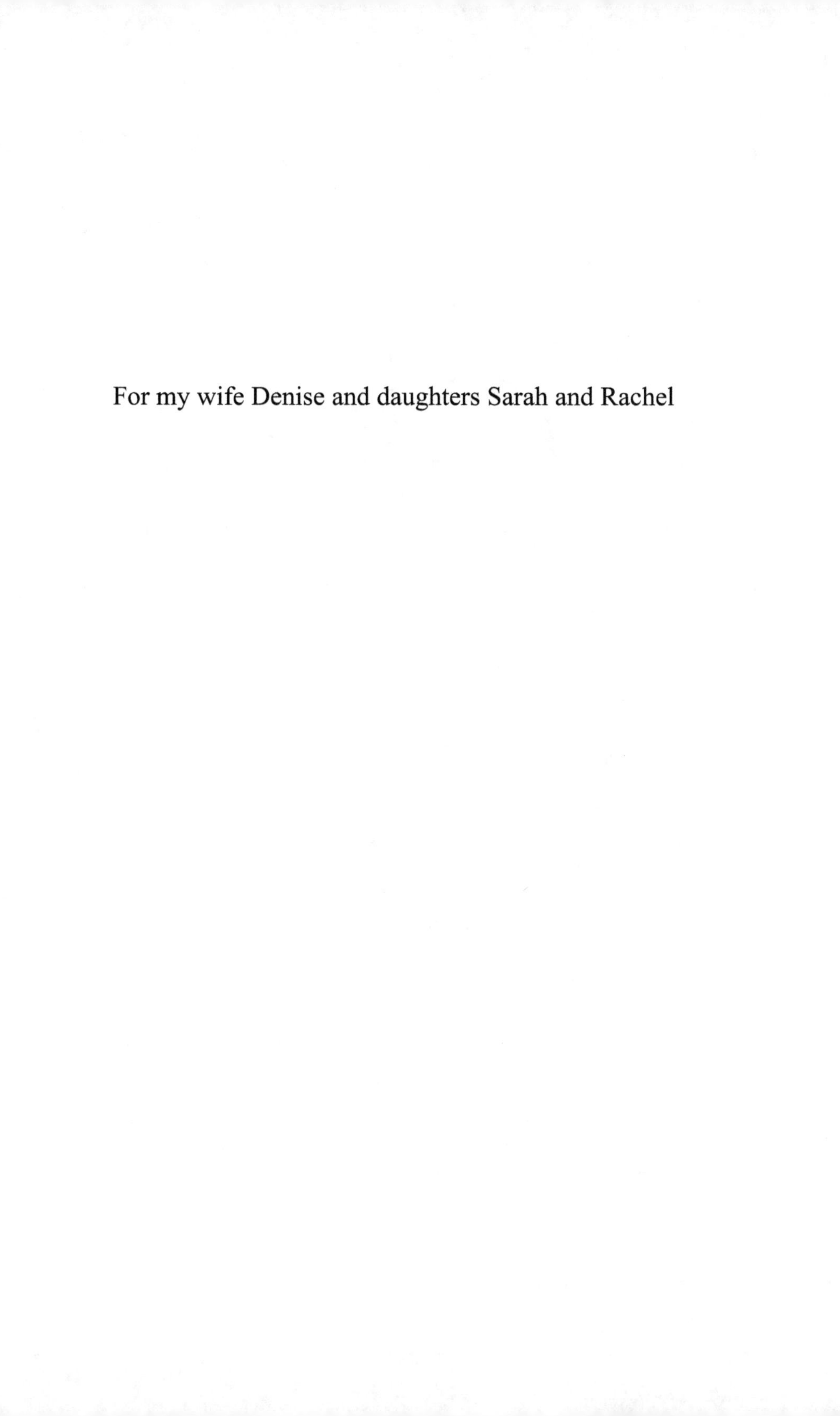

For my wife Denise and daughters Sarah and Rachel

Acknowledgments

I am grateful for the advice and support from my family, colleagues, and teachers who made this book possible. I would especially like to thank David Ervin, editor-in-chief, and Randy Brown, poetry editor of the Military Experience and the Arts *(As You Were),* and Tina Hacker, poetry editor for the Veterans Voices Writing Project (*Veterans' Voices),* for their willingness to give access to my poems through publication. And special thanks to Rachel Breitweser for her copy-editing overview.

Thank you as well to the following publications, where versions of these poems previously appeared:

As You Were: The Military Review: "I-Was-There Award"

Veterans' Voices: "Veteran's Day," "SGT Kelley," "Borderland of Peace Seeking," "Scud Hole"

Contents

Glossary

6x6 - three-axle vehicle; usually all-wheel drive
AFN - American Forces Network
AFTH - Air Force Theater Hospital
Anbar Province - region of Iraq to the west of Baghdad
Apache - AH-64 attack helicopter
Black Hawk - UH-60 utility helicopter
C-17 - Globemaster III transport aircraft
C-130 - Hercules transport aircraft
CHU - Conex Housing Units
CID - military Criminal Investigation Division
CIF - Central Issue Facility for military equipment
Click - one kilometer
CO - Commanding Officer
Concertina - coiled razor wire that expands like a concertina
CONEX - military shipping container (Container Express)
CONUS - Continental United States
DFAC - Dining Facility
Downrange - area where soldiers are deployed; a combat zone
Dust-off - callsign for helicopter casualty evacuation
FUBAR - F*cked Up Beyond All Recognition
Gatling - multiple revolving barrel machine gun
Green Zone - heavily fortified zone in central Baghdad
Gyrenes - slang term for someone in the U.S. Marine Corps
Hau - fast-growing tree found in Hawaii
Haboob - term derived from Arabic for intense dust storm
Hercules, herky-birds - see C-130
HQ - Headquarters
IED - Improvised Explosive Device
JDAMs, JSOWs, GBUs, SLAMs - acronyms for weapons
Kalama - beach park on Kailua Bay, Oahu
Katyusha - common term for a wide range of artillery rockets
KBR - military contractor for logistical and operational support
LT - Lieutenant
M9, mike-9 - Beretta semiautomatic 9mm pistol
MASCAL - Mass-Casualty situation

Mortaritaville - military base that is regularly attacked; Balad AFB
MOS - Military Occupational Specialty
MP - Military Police
MP5 - Heckler & Koch 9mm submachine gun
MSG - Master Sergeant
NCOIC - Non-Commissioned Officer in Charge
Nine-line - military request for combat injury medevacs
North Shore - northern beach area of Oahu
ODS - Operation Desert Storm, followed Operation Desert Shield
OIC - Officer in Charge
Olomana - windward Oahu mountain
Optempo - Operations Tempo
PCOS - Permanent Change of Station move
Phalanx Gatling - radar-controlled Gatling gun
Predator - armed military unmanned aerial vehicle
PX - Post Exchange
R&R - Rest and Recuperation
Rad - term for radiologist
Repo - someone who replaces another soldier
ROE - Rules of Engagement
Sandbox - military slang for deployment in a desert
Scud - Soviet-era tactical ballistic missiles used by Iraq
SGT - Sergeant
SNAFU - Situation Normal, All F*cked Up
Spectre - heavily-armed AC-130 ground-attack aircraft
Strike Eagles - F-15E dual-role fighter
Super Hornets - F/A-18E/F attack aircraft
Theater - military area of operations
Top - term for unit's senior NCOIC
Torus gantry - ring shaped part of CT scanner
UCMJ - Uniform Code of Military Justice
USO - United Service Organization
Viper - later variant of F-16 Fighting Falcon
Warthog - A-10 low-flying tank killer

I-Was-There Award

Weeks before Shield became Storm,
join combat hospital in Bahrain. CO
greets: not much use for you right
now, grab shovel and fill sandbags.
Really? We're Army here, all pull
together for hospital success. As a
medical corps officer, expect to
contribute, lead by example,
eat last.

Wander out to sandpile where
sandbag-detail sarge takes charge,
shows how to shovel fill bag to proper
heft, while maintaining moldability.
After several awkward attempts, get
precise way to tie off bag so secure,
but single tug releases knot to spill
sand. Perform task day-after-day
until the night the great air armada
passes overhead, heralding onset
of hostility.

Relief short lived, no casualty
x-rays to interpret. Go stack bags
3 high around tents to keep rain out
when comes. During days of aerial
destruction of armor vehicles dug-in,
burying Iraqi soldiers terrified in
trenches beyond sand berms who
wave white, futile, surrender flags to
ugly strafing warthogs, pile bags
3 high around each tent until
job properly done.

When ground war begins, dash to
battle station for x-rays to interpret,
grateful release from sandbags, able
now to execute duty here to fulfill.
Standby 100 hours, all it took before
war's end. Expected POWs? All
cared for by Muslim-field units.

Mission complete for hospital: ordered
strike tents, prepare to leave. CO tasks
to take care them plump-olive sandbags.
Labor in midday sun, stack sandbags on
pallets head high. Realize while sweat
drips, best paid bag stacker anywhere.
Stack 'em wide, stack 'em tall, then

home to I-Was-There award.

GulfWarBowl I

Whitney's soaring anthem stokes
jingoistic SuperBowl XXV crowd,
while Coach Stormin' Norman's aerial
assault preps the field for GM Bush's
half-million players ready to rip
into Coach Saddam's team.

Spring coiled along lines of departure,
aggrieved veterans of the VietnamGame,
eager to reclaim honor, impatiently wait
through the devastating bombardment,
ducking Saddam's sporadic feeble Scud
retorts. Forty days, time to get it on.

Ground offense roars forward, rolls over
the ragged defense, thrust into the endzone.
Still eager to push on, decimate Saddam to
avert a GulfWarBowl II, but GM Bush
says enough's enough, come home to
a grateful nation. God bless.

In winning locker rooms, rides home,
welcoming parades, VietnamGame
veterans hug, shed tears, redeemed.
Able now to retire with heads held high:
their fairy-tale achievement 'til the next
mendacious event.

Escape SFO USO

Sleepwalk in on pre-dawn
airport shuttle, radio reports
stricken WTC north tower.

Arrive SFO bustle for Boston
flight, walk to gate as monitors
announce all flights ground stop.

South tower struck, FAA prohibits
foreseeable future flights. SFO USO
beckons: crowded refuge where

worried eyes peer at images, gasp
as towers grinding crumble spawn
dust clouds, the harbinger of war.

Trapped in crowded uncertainly:
yesterday's destinations discarded,
tomorrow's journeys yet unforetold.

Restless writhe on reclining chairs,
while talking heads struggle to make
sense of incomprehensible acts.

Calls to commander elicit
no answers, told stand-by
until more is known.

SFO USO imprisoned
until pizza delivery sneaks in
at dusk, reveals path out.

Escape at dawn, taxi to city
replete with empty hotels, cafés
begging come hinter and feast

while awaiting passage.
Life on hold by fate; soon
to ruck-up, deploy.

Dread

Are we afraid?
Concerned misfortune may
come our way downrange?
Having sudden bursts of dread:
are sandbox's mean streets worse

than monster rigs that devour
rearview mirrors, crotch jockeys
that split lanes, honking SUVs
that erupt on-and-off crisscross
entrances and exits.

More dangerous than
North Shore's booming surf, or
undertow that sucks the unwary, or
tumbling off rain-slick Olomana trails.
Screaming as sightseer 'copter plunges
to earth, or everyday danger of simply
biking bike lanes.

Does greater danger in Green Zone lurk?
Sanctuary to merchandise crammed PXs,
greasy burger joints, oily swimming pools.
Where sporadic rockets or mortar rounds
vault over walls coiled razor-wire crowned.

On homeland's mean streets,
injury or death results from reckless
neglect. Downrange, trauma's the outcome
of deliberate intent to maim or kill: the
shock of mortar's blast inside the wire,
bewilderment when a rocket's blast erupts
outside DFAC disrupting breakfast.

All indirect but voluntary fire.
Not specifically for us: if we're hit, fine;
if not, that's also okay. Who are these
surreptitious others seeking to harm or kill?
Shadowy bombardiers rarely exposed.

Screaming for Truth

Screaming-for-Truth tribe,
Stars and Stripes says,
lobs Katyusha rockets
over Tigris into the zone.

Cease when chief's grandchild's
life saved in our Green Zone hospital.
Cessation the expression of gratitude,
end of violence mercy's reward.

Green Zone Briefing

First and only
briefing upon
arrival at Green
Zone hospital.

Don't flush your
toilet paper; wad
it up, stuff it in an
empty H2O bottle.

Screw this up, and
you'll be tracked
down through DNA
analysis of pipe

clogging tissue;
your name forever
posted on the latrine
wall of shame.

Hubris Checkmate

Trained soldiers, sergeant major growls,
standing tall, leaning forward, mission ready,
too long delayed. General wants us in-country,
now, where needed. Get us on a flight!

Enlisted grunt, ramrod straight: sir!
adverse weather thwarts all flights.
Blustery gusts whap and snap the
air-base's cavernous liaison tent;
Satan's sandstorm rages, the fierce
solar antipode of winter blizzard.

Scorching desert gusts shred,
like blizzard's howling icy blast;
gritty driven sand abrades,
like raw, frozen sleet;
sand fog embraces and cloaks,
like hoarfrost; desert sand
sheet streams over tarmac
and drift piles like snow
against the woven-wire fence.

Gust driven ground grit pierces
olive, coarse-woven bandanas
knotted low behind necks,
excoriating roughened skin,
coating mucus membranes
as slick as the frozen condensation
of blizzard's exhaled breath.

Just a fricking haboob! Sergeant major
scowls toward lashed down, sandblasted,
herky-birds that squat forlorned.
Fought through this crap in '91!

Caresses taro-leaf combat patch of
"First to Fight!" mechanized division
whose infantry fighting vehicles, tanks
ripped and decimated republican guards.

Now stands proud on desert battleground
once dominated by his lethal skill, but
by Satan's capricious blizzard, the
sergeant major is wind whipped.

Sometimes We Cry

I.

ODS charter touches Arabian
Peninsula as sun kisses horizon.
Assemble on tarmac alongside
sprawling, drab duffle-bag mound,
until NCOIC deems it sufficiently
dark, turns loose rodents to scurry
in futile search by feeble red-lens
light to locate, retrieve our four.
Claw, push, elbow, curse in our
frantic search for gear; the

charter crew slam hatches, 747
taxies, rumbles off ascending
twinkling star sky, follows setting
sun home. Watch its winking
lights extinguish our final link
home. Despair descends to
envelop the uncertainty of
our bleak prospect of ever
returning home.

II.

Pristina charter runway stranded:
recline, plug in earbuds, dial tune.
Burl Ives warns of the blue tail fly,
"Jimmy crack corn and I don't care."

Divert to Skopje where met with no
basic-ammo issue. Midnight convoy
through Kosovar mountain-forest

roads to Camp Bondsteel. Soldiers'
vulnerable trek stripped of fire and
autonomy; only control music
selection and bobbing heads.

III.

Baghdad journey starts herky-jerky.
Back from departure gate, short taxi,
abrupt stop, engines shutdown until
hours delayed departure to Kuwait.
Surrender as fantasy grip of freewill
slips away. After snack, glass of wine,
sleep from Cape Cod to Black Sea.

Skirting Syrian spike, request final
glass of wine to flatter curried rice.
Sorry, alcohol not allowed: sacred
religious restraint reaches into sky,
sealing freedom's loss.

Sandstorm delays flight to Baghdad;
Internet café's wireless access's down,
satellite problem, could be the server;
vending machine spits out phone card
with smudged, unreadable numbers.

Head to pool for Zen lap stroking.
Van Morrison murmurs in our ears:
"Sometimes we cry." Who cares,
in the slow lane, no one sees
our tears.

Tithing of Children

Toddler girl dust-off
air-drops into our combat hospital;
injuries courtesy of errant mortar round
that plunged into guileless child's
courtyard seclusion.

Strapped unto the CT scanner
that shelter-hunkers outside; its
pedestal slaughterhouse-vestment draped,
cloaked to absorb the blood and fluids that
spurt, leak, spill from her ravaged, shattered
body cradled on the floating table as she
glides through the plump torus gantry;
where invisible, rotating, razor-thin,
ionizing radiation briskly bandsaws
her from crown to pubis.

Penetrating, revealing the ill-fated ravage of war;
nothing sacred to escape the healers' gaze.
Lewdly exposed battered, disrupted abdominal organs
foretell her future: despite frantic struggle,
she dies shortly after arrival.

Alone, without family, because
her mother had already succumbed to
injuries en route to our combat hospital.
Little daughter's name never learnt:
known only by her trauma ID number.

First Sunday morning in-country,
first of many to come.

On yet another desolate night,
midtrimester Madonna wept
in the CT scanner as it scans
her fecund abdomen, divulging a
supine fetus sprawled alongside the
intruding, metallic shard that pierced
the uterine wall.

Fetal hands, uplifted in the
draining fluid of the breached womb,
beseech the gods to halt the madness.
But on this night in our combat hospital,
the right-to-life gods are off-duty.

We slouch afterwards outside
in the predawn glow, smoking,
drinking coffee, headshaking
over sectarian clashes demanding
such slaughter. Reverie disturbed
by Black Hawk's arrival full of
fresh casualties. Musings checked,
scrambled 'til latest consignment
triaged, scanned, sorted, treated,
'til relief replacements arrive.

Past recollections flee as rad tech
hastily rushes in. IED, child casualties,
critical needs trauma scan now. Lights
flipped on, key strikes enter protocols.
Phone rings, answered, listens, hangs up;
shuts scan room lights off, turns to say:
critical expired in the trauma bay.

And so it goes . . .

Latrine Lock

Greenhorn, repo shadow gazer joins
Green Zone combat hospital already
six months on-station. Eager and anxious,
are we up to the task? Fit for the game?
Await first MASCAL to truly know.

Roused from sleep by jangling phone,
presence in ER urgently needed, inbound
casualties requiring scans. Having slept
in camouflage fatigues, need only lace
on boots, rush to chaotic ER full of
shouts, commands, and demands.

Jitters grips, need to piss, duck into
latrine to gain relief. Now into the
ruckus, but damn, cannot get door
to unlock! Outside hear din swell
as casualties pour in, above all:
where's rad doc, need urgent CT!

Struggle, but fricking door won't release!
Turn and twist lock's knob over and again,
but no joy. Lock refuses to yield! Oh the
ignominy, trapped in a latrine during
first MASCAL.

Hear urgent, angry voices, where's he?
Call him! Phone buzzes, jiggles in pocket;
desperately try harder to open the door,
but lock won't relent. Last desperate act,
turn lock knob beyond expected point
of breaking; it turns without resistance
and door pops open when handle's
depressed.

Precious lesson learned:
half turn right closes,
turn and a half left opens.
Easy in, hard to get out.

Ying Yang of Call

Soldiers patrolling outside the wire in
this hellhole city, caught in factional
rage. First soldier's rifle-fire struck, swift
mean-street sacrifice; another's penetrating
head wound hastens to the ER for CT scan,
so surgeons can plot trauma repairs. But
scan reveals a wound deemed expectant.

The company commander learns of
the scan's foretelling of imminent death,
slumps, weeps, head bowed between knees.
Disconsolate elder brother of vanquished
young brethren. Sons and lovers entrusted
by women from distant homes for safekeeping;
who know not yet the heartbreak that
soon visits from foreign land.

In an adjacent trauma bay lies a soldier
who arrived complaining of chest pain
after rocket's nearby burst. CT scan
displays jagged shrapnel that punched
through outer chest wall lining, laying
on the inner lining of collapsing lung.

He claims he's shaving when struck:
we laugh at this most bizarre shaving-cut
story ever. But an irreverent, yet more
observant ER nurse exclaims: look at the
penetration angle! You were bent over,
taking a shit when struck, weren't you.
A Purple Heart wound to rejoice about.

The Mother of All . . .

"The mother of all battles!"
declares the brutal dictator.
Does Saddam enflame our
Arabic-speaking guard,
crouched with an MP5
adjacent to the TV?

While we warily
perch on our couches
with puny holstered M9s
and listen to the delayed
English interpretation.

We wonder, as Saddam's
rant unveils on the screen,
will our protector heed
his contracted bond, or
the ancient desert bond.

SGT Kelley

I see you ogling my lanky athletic beauty,
my cropped-brindle hair brushed and glossy.
My dark eyes track your reckless approach,
and yes, that's my tongue that drapes and
drools over fanged teeth as I pant in the
suffocating Iraqi heat, sprawled here in

the enclosed hold of a C-130-night flight
to Bagdad. Do upright ears, narrow chest
betray my Belgian Malinois heritage?
I'm SGT Kelley, military working dog.
That kickass corporal over there, who calls
himself my handler, he works for me,

not I for him. He exists only to ensure my
safety and survival. When I burn my paw pads
on the scorched hard ball while out on patrol,
the big lunk picks me up and carries me. I'm
sure I got heavy after a couple clicks. If roaming
ferals threaten attack, he employs lethal force

to protect me. But his show of true devotion
came last mission when special ops requested
a dog to sweep for unexploded ordnance. That's
my MOS, sniffing out explosives. So we Black
Hawk in, link up with the cowboys. No sooner
set down, an incoming round knocks me

flat. When I pop back up, corporal sees
that I'm bleeding from shrapnel wounds.
She's wounded! He shouts, pressing bandages
to stem the blood flow. Call the nine-line!
Lead cowboy balks at his dust-off request;
still wants me to perform the sweep!

No can do, you bastards! She's out of here!
Dust-off evacs me to a battalion aid station
for wound suturing and Purple Heart pinning.
Our C-130 descends, touches down, taxies to
terminal. After this short layover, I'm off
to USA for well-deserved R&R leave.

Corporal stays, he'll team up with another
dog. They don't want us forming close bonds,
which leads to bad habits. I'm okay with that,
though I'll never forget he saved this dog's ass.
I'll soon return for 'nother tour, then retire
when old, if I survive Iraq's mean streets.

Simple Request

Hands blown off, wrists
cauterized by the intense heat,
the insurgent bombmaker
leans forward murmuring
over and again a phrase.
What does he want?

Is he in pain? Does he
implore Allah for relief?
No, says Arabic 'terp, he
says kill him now 'cause
he doesn't want anyone
else wiping his ass.

Sandbox Showers

Hot water's tepid,
but the cold water
is sure to scald.
Welcome to the
sandbox mobile
shower trailers.

And don't be
shocked when
showering proves
electrifying. Some-
times they're just
wired that way.

Haircut Doggerel

US barber cloaks in silky shawl,
your back to mirror as they buzz
away hair to preference. All the
while talking 'bout them Yankees.
Until spun, wah-lah! Rejoice
in the magic of their chore.
Not so in Arabia,

where seated gaze into the mirror.
Mike-9 clutched under slippery
shroud, finger strokes the trigger
as barber strops blade to razor
glide crescents above the ears.
Both rejoice at haircut's finale,
each alive another day.

Combat Hospital Mascot

Children gunshot, or raging infection,
broken bones poking through skin,
congenital ailment deforming a smile,
horrific disfiguring cookfire burn.

All abandoned at downrange
combat hospitals' front gates.

Mysterious arrivals in the night,
to be found at dawning light,
discarded for crushing tribes'
resources, resolve, and charity.
No farewell note, or
way to contact family.

Castoffs, suffering children of war.
Mute seekers of refuge. Taken in,
compassionate staff swaddle,
assign nicknames to adoptees.

Though children's medical or
surgical ailments stretch the
scope of combat hospitals,
staff improvise care because
children cannot go to CONUS,
nor to impoverished host nation
hospitals whose care is
fraught with danger.

These war orphans healed by
the training, skill, experience, and
meds, surgical gear surreptitiously
smuggled downrange by replacements
as old staff rotate home.

Reluctant caregiver handoffs,
treatment plans carefully outlined,
further surgeries laid out.
Embrace your downrange
hospital mascot.

Scud Hole

Gape into the mesmerizing crater
where oily, brackish water collects,
covering its bottom,
disguising the depth
to which the Scud blasted

a chasm where the DFAC once sat,
where we routinely congregated
to consume meals often interrupted
by the prophetic wailing sirens
of impending calamity.

Orwellian Gobbledygook

Black Hawks swoop low over the
sand-berm barrier of Camp Bucca's
desert prison. Insurgents confined by
concertina hunch under our rotor blast.
We crabwalk out under rotating blades;
hospital top tosses our gear in truck,
drives us to in-process.

Discover *1984* the bureaucracy exemplar:
Not prison, Detention Temporary
Incarceration Facility.
Not prisoner, detainee.
Orwellian gobbledygook!

Alarms alert when detainee self-releases.
You mean escape? Don't call it escape;
say detainee self-releases.
We laugh and top laughs, too.
Orwell also laughs over language
mangled to shape thoughts,
control actions.

Detainees' legal status?
Sovereign citizens held by occupiers?
Or detainees of host government?

No one knows for sure, yet uncertainty
breeds no angst among medicos who
assuage detainee afflictions within
the inside-the-wire infirmary:
just patients needing care. Grateful,

but mind sign's warnings:
Remain alert! Restrain patients!
Don't turn your back on them;
maintain situational awareness;
where's the guard!

Yes, just here to treat 'em as
patients. No need to get involved
in process or politics. What about
abuse or torture? If I saw or heard
something, report it up the chain
of command, I'm sure I would.

Interrogation? What about that?
Need to join in? No, though some do.
Only observe to ensure detainee
safety during harsh questioning.
Try not to interfere 'cause

more concerned about our
guard tower MPs, who require
frequent admissions for acute
depression. Driven by despair,
reaction to ethical challenges?
No, boredom; want to be
out kicking down doors,
detaining insurgents.

Scary Things

Murmuring voices sift through
concertina crowned chain-link
fences; imposing guard towers
control interlocking fields-of-fire;
detainees languish indeterminately.

Outside the pen, ordinary people live
downrange in white-trash trailers; stride
along crunchy gravel paths to latrine or
shower tents, set among blast barriers,
duck-and-cover shelters; dodge trucks
coming and going on potholed roads;
numbed by monotonous, throbbing drone
of fume-spurting diesel generators. Also
imprisoned in concertina hurricane fences:
fields of fire directed outward.

Ordinary people: guards trading restraining tips
for detainees with golfers' casual dispassion, but
instead of using big drivers to carry par 5 hole,
use Brazilian Jiujitsu to restrain unruly big guy.
Dining shrinks offhandedly chat about helping
interrogators break down detainees, as if
comparing effective child-rearing techniques.
Ordinary people, everyday practices.

Not all jailers are our countrymen. Bulgarians,
camped next door, smoke first cigarettes of the
day, drink coffee outside their tents. We greet
them: Bulgarian comrades, loyal conscripts of
dwindling coalition of willing; good morning!
They laugh, offer cigarettes. What do you do?
They reply, don't know. How long you here?
Again, don't know. Fellow captives of
capricious folly, freedom lost.

Not all so cheerful. Iraqi-Kurd interpreter,
an emigrant to Colorado after the 1st Persian
Gulf War, concedes conditions have improved
here somewhat. Must believe in Iraq's future to
willingly return, given that Arabic interpreters
so often killed. Not really, do this because no
work at home; left family for contract. We're
all mercenaries, migrant sandbox workers.

Despite drawn out occupation, going outside
wire still forbidden. Scary enough inside with
'copters swooping in, fighters roaring overhead,
distant rifle fire, sporadic explosive booming.
Scariest of all harsh braying Phalanx Gatling
guns' response to radar detected incoming fire.
Local wisdom: sound of Gatling fire and no
explosion, good; sound of Gatling fire and
explosion, bad.

Real, over-the-top scariness came one day when
dusk entices a stroll. Long story short, miss
cutoff, walk and, as it gets darker and darker,
almost walk through wire's gate into free-fire
country! Stopped by guards who, when asked
where are we, respond, in Iraq! As if that's not
obvious from the first step off the spaceship
into this sandbox.

Three-stripe sergeant sent to fetch us back
wonders what we're looking for out here.
Progress. What? He looks quite perplexed.
Explain that before departing home kept
hearing progress was being made in Iraq.
He laughs, shakes head: you'll not find it
over there or anywhere in-country
for that matter.

Paintball War

Perfect ski-resort setting! proclaims
visiting grandee, outstretched arms
embrace exquisite, piney-emerald rugged
mountain bowl that encircles Bagram.

Better clear mountains of mines
planted during decades of war,
Afghan interpreter suggests. Three
years ago, passenger plane crashed
in those mountains. Two soldiers died
stepping on mines trying to recover victims.

Ski resort indeed. Mines and moguls;
enchanting only the extreme,
off-piste skiers.

Only see 500 clicks out, nothing after that
but fog, briefs the local PowerPoint ranger.
Tactics to pacify Taliban in Hindu Kush
shadow swing like a weather vane in the
election outcome winds.

At the DFAC, the don't-salute-me,
work-for-a-living sergeant kvetches
about how much taxpayers shell out
each day to KBR contractor for meals!
The former 'Bama school teacher on a
kitchen-work contract boasts about making
each year what she made in ten teaching!
All living the dream.

Of course, insurgent attacks grab
everyone's attention; we're isolated,
so we're a tempting target. Thus,
command devised a defense strategy:

all assigned military pull guard duty
with strict rules-of-engagement that
deliberately escalate whenever
Afghans approach the gate.

Guards first challenge
by holding up hands and yelling:
No! No! No! As if the person
approaching is a two-year-old.
Get it? Yeah, we get it.

If they continued their approach,
we shoot them with paintball guns!
Just like teenagers playing wargames?

Although hard to believe,
lethal force is only authorized after
engaging with paintballs first.

So, jokes the visiting grandee, if we see
someone paint splattered inside the wire,
we're authorized to kill them?
Yes, you are.

Top-Dog Doc

See the Afghan Army top-dog doc
in wood-paneled office resplendent;
wants CT scanners and ultrasonography,
but scrutiny of medical-maintenance cubicle
reveals only pliers, screwdrivers, and hammers
not adequate to maintain cutting-edge machinery.

Meanwhile, NATO-medical logisticians scramble
to execute burgeoning budgets
to purchase pills, bandages, medical paraphernalia
to stuff warehouses overflowing
whose padlocked doors unlock only
to keys on top-dog doc's keychain.

Hard Landing

Hercules departs Baghdad International;
immediately after wheels up, loses power;
pilot executes 180, perfect level-wing
"landing" in barren field adjacent airport.

According to Reuters, no sign of enemy fire
or damage to airframe. C-130 still airworthy?
Not so, according to passengers who describe
wheels ripped off, gaping holes in fuselage.

USAF insists, despite violated airframe integrity,
this is a hard landing, not crash. Doesn't look like
an airframe to jack up, replace blown tires, fly again.
Like Humpty-Dumpty, ain't goin' rise up no more.

Hard landing label distorts reality. Orwellian jargon
hoodwinks, manipulated language that misconstrues
"don't call it a crash." White lies make us skeptics
no longer able to discern truth from fiction.

Java Hut

Showtime on Mosul flight line.
Told at required early arrival our
flight's delayed a couple hours.
No surprise since sandbox flights
often delayed. Time to waste,
cater to caffeine-comfort crave.
Perch near Java Hut door, see
faint haze on evening breeze.

We sniff the smoke that tinges the air.
It's shit, infantry grunt says, squatting
near barrier, lighting a cigarette. Are
you from the hospital? We visited there
for the last couple days. Probably your
shit they're burning now, over by the
old Monastery; they do it every night.
Crushes cigarette, enters Java Hut.

Soldiers come and go, coffee
purchased before going outside the
wire on patrol; their casual swagger
of handling weapons hints lethal
expertise with war instruments.
Peaceful dusk as day's end light
fades, the emerging least moon
hovers over darkening airfield.

More soldiers arrive with travel
gear; good sign promised flight
soon arrives? No, flight controller
says: flight now departs at midnight.
Offers alternate 'copter flight to Tikrit,

get us there by midnight, try to work
us unto the manifest. But we're not
optimistic, too many times we've
been burned by Catfish Air.

Predator drone taxies to active runway;
engine revs like an outboard with prop
out of water, lifts off, labors skyward.
Harsh buzz, flashing strobe, marks path
from Java Hut. Elevation achieved,
turns south as strobe light winks off,
engine throttles to muted hum. Only
to be replaced by nearby startling
rattle of automatic-weapon fire.

Making sure crew-operated weapons
good-to-go after clearing gate, says
three-striper, back with fragrant brew.
Weapon fire from rangers who earlier
stopped at Java Hut? Nods, slurps coffee,
descends steps to roundabout where a
dusty, battered, up-armored Humvee
pauses to pick him up.

Half hour later, taxiing C-130, its approach
and landing undetected in least moon light,
the blacked-out aircraft only followed on
dark taxiway by propwash that reverberates,
reflects off hangers until it halts, drops ramp
to reveal itself offloading soldiers and cargo.
Noisy engines idle, eager for fast departure.
Not going where you want,
says flight controller.

Two helicopters whomp-whomp in;
rough men exit Black Hawk while
others stand by to board. Though
coveted Black Hawk rides, at rollcall
only gunslingers gathered gear. Was
wrong, controller confesses, can't
squeeze you on rotary-wing flights.
Slouch back in chair, continue to
wait for flight long delayed.

After Black Hawks gone, throttled
jet whine of aircraft on final approach;
shortly thereafter, engine reversers thunder,
slowing landed craft. When it approaches,
interior lights through open ramp lights up
C-17 tail. Turbine howl blocks conversation
as controller rushes past: point to aircraft,
to us, shakes head no.

Forklifts scurry, offload, load pallets.
Passengers neither exit nor enter loitering
C-17. Arrived from outside sandbox, now
another country bound. Last pallet on, rear
ramp closes, lights extinguish, C-17 retreats
into night. Follow engine whine as taxies out
to runway; takeoff run revealed by dark shape
blinking out dim lights from distance hills.

Hush cloaks the field after bustle of action.
C-130 flight now projected other side of midnight.
Shrug it off, wrap in poncho liner to ward off chill.
Expect delays after air-jacking around sandbox.

Travel reality: although we're the occupying force,
the insurgents control the roads. Ground travel
too dangerous, even for a few miles.
Air travel's a necessity.

Jolt awake well after midnight when C-130
arrives. Time to ruck up, hump gear onboard.
Preboard ritual: jam earplugs into canals;
clasp-lock, tight-cinch Kevlar helmet;
ballistic-glasses bows slide inside straps;
struggle into 40 lbs. body armor; hump 55 lbs.
duffle bag onto back, snug down straps.
Last, pick up 35 lbs. backpack that holds
precious laptop.

Sweat sheens skin as join file of soldiers
on tarmac apron. Waved forward, bent
under idling turboprop exhaust, searing
like an opened oven's exhale. Flight crew
grasp our hand, pulls 300 lbs. swinging-dick
one huge step-up into aircraft. Move forward
shrug off gear, plop weary ass on canvas seat,
lean helmet back against web-strap
fuselage lining.

Hope for empty seat across way to cradle
weary feet. Crew web restrains duffels, close
ramp; C-130 taxis to runway and no pause,
max power take-off. Wheels up, but remain
low over field gathering speed to ascend,
bobbing and weaving, for one hour flight.
When arrive Balad, exit reversal of entry.
Later that day we'll wish we had more
coffee from the Java Hut.

Hunker Down

Gazing through the hospital portals,
we're hoodwinked into a vison of Mars
as the luminous afternoon rays dissipate
through rust tarnished, wispy talc dust.

Reluctant to venture outside, we savor
this sanctuary shelter, particularly during
the utter panic of frequent broadcast
alarms, warning of incoming fire.

Our hospital's blessed with a megabuck
Kevlar protective shield that hovers
above, providing safe harbor for wise
souls who linger, loath to depart for
off-duty time in thin-wall canvas tents.

We seek hunker-down schemes between
shifts to squander time: exercise, games,
watching films, cruising the Internet. Or
become addicted sports junkies, soap opera/
gameshow buffs. Whatever ticks the clock
faster until back to work, then home.

When first arrive, intent on acquiring new
talent, we fail to grasp the need for torpor.
Shouldn't seek novelty as distraction
where too much stimulus already exists;
instead seek detachment to assuage horror
of bodies torn apart. Guitar or banjo
mastery also not the balm, dissonant chords
annoy tentmates seeking sleep. Still,

our most fateful sin is our refusal to accept that hunkering down leads to an ill-fated mindset of thoughtlessly embraced routines, which saps willingness for bold actions. We become placeholders, clock punchers, shift fillers, plodders.

Doing time, making no difference, not rocking the boat. Never trying something new or setting in motion anything that has to be completed before we can go home. After all, we're going home win or lose.

Where's the Comfort Zone

Never worked with electronic medical
record before, gripes the newly arrived
reserve psychologist. Maybe I can jot down
some notes, someone else transcribe? Like
private practice, won't need a computer.

Activated to provide mental health
solace for Anbar Province Gyrenes,
back home treats only attention deficit
kids. No experience talking programmed
killers out of suicide!

What can we say, but welcome here.

Desolate, daunting, hostile base, at
O-dark-early he steps out of CONEX
sleeping cave to stumble on gravel into an
ankle brace. Barely able to locate Green Bean
coffee shop within the blast-wall maze.

Always dodging trail-bike gorillas:
body armor clad; Kevlar helmets
night-vision optics adorned; assault
carbine slung, magazines replete.
A Monty Python skit?!

He complains to clinic OIC 'cause commanders
call, demand to be told which indoctrinated killer
seeks counseling.

OIC reminds frustrated therapist that reg
says to keep company commanders informed
about the health of fighters, especially
all things mental.

What about privacy? He worries Gyrenes who
seek therapy may be seen as disciplinary glitches.

Retorts OIC: if company command demands info,
there's no privacy. If Gyrenes want privacy,
send them to chaplains.

Newbie angers OIC who's
already installed a discrete entry to
the mental health clinic to entice visits
away from commanders' prying eyes;
not wanting another regretful, lingering,
overdose death.

Most superbly skilled reservist medicos
survive their boots-on-ground duty, which
later spawn tales told over cold ones of being
pumped after MASCAL exploits, like winners
of company softball tournaments.

Yet, some struggle,
similar to the requested but
whiny therapist, when yanked from
their comfort zone.

Time to get your head out of your ass!
Be the solution, not the problem.
Stiffen your back!

Waiting Game

Gyrenes wait in formation, wait for orders,
wait sprawled on floor for transports to arrive,
wait sweltering in helmets, body armor to depart,
wait in armored vehicles to go outside the wire,
wait for something to happen, when it happens,
wait for it to stop so they can come back inside.

Sometimes wait for buddies to live or die.
All the time forever waiting to go home.
Waiting's hard, not all do it well; not all
figure out ways to fill time. They joined for
the adventure, fulfillment none experienced
at home. They're

the few, the proud, who joined so authority figures
would tell them what to do, when to do it; they're
the ones who lacked respected parents, friends, teachers
in their homes, neighborhoods, schools from whom
they'd willingly take direction.

Gyrenes exude discipline; sit straight-backed
at chow, assault weapons strapped across chest
ready to engage. Always ready to fight; every
movement a combat patrol. Formation assembles
under high-noon sun, execute Drill-and-Ceremony.
Order, peer worship, the way of life. Cut adrift by
a reduced optempo that's unwelcomed.

Waiting's wasted time, don't like wasting time.
No need now to go outside the wire; now too
much time at hand, too much time to think.
Waiting bears down hard, lacks meaning,
not real; want something to bring purpose;

unable to find worthwhile diversions. Too
much of that challenge out in the real world;
joined the Corps to bring structure to lives.

But LT wants Gyrenes to get rest, enjoy
free-time, get ready for next time. Games,
movies, music, sports distract for a while, then
want some more excitement. Only so much
eating, exercising, watching, listening,
sleeping before becoming a treadmill
of tedious monotony.

Days of waiting can be the ticket to crazy.
Some act out, often declared flareups
of preexisting mental disorders bubbling
to the surface; not reactions to stress endured.

Even the most balanced get overwhelmed
when stress challenges. Thus, on any given
night, distressed Gyrenes occupy hospital beds:
some needing meds to take the jittery edge off,
others suicidal. They'll be evacuated before
their Anbar Province deployment ends,
their waiting game over.

Cost Benefit Ratio

Vipers Roman candle heavenward,
hunters' bomb ladened search for
shoot-and-scoot insurgent rocketeers
arching Katyusha rockets into
Mortaritaville.

Strike Eagles' afterburners flare,
rip the Bagram night. Wings bristle
with armament to rain death-from-
above on Pashto-Taliban snipers,
rare return with racks burdened.

Warthog Gatling guns snarl;
Apache's a hovering executioner;
Spectre gunship discharges kickass 105s;
sea launched Super Hornets dispense
JDAMs, JSOWs, GBUs, and SLAMs.

Surgical strikes destroy targets, neutralize.
Show of force to deter jihadi attacks against
the coalition, or so claims official doctrine.
Our champagne responses to beer budget
attacks; dollars for us, pennies for them.

Talk to Me

In wars before, a hurried letter scribbled
during combat pause, overlooking a river
valley, dark forest, next island to storm.
Don't worry, quiet here; soon rotate for
R&R. Words that arrive late, doubling
the heartbreak after news we've already
bought and paid for the farm.

Sometime no letter comes from Tarawa,
Peleliu jungle, frozen Chosin reservoir,
Khe Sanh. Survival only by blocking
loved ones from thoughts; consumed by
horrific grind getting through another night,
another day, the next 87. Until promised
rotation home. Sorry, can't bear writing.

First time on Arabian Peninsula, call home
courtesy US telecom. Ten bucks a minute,
lucky get five; stand in line an hour for that.
Great to hear your voices in real time; recorded
tape exchanges nice but banter lags.

Second tour, ringing cell phone interrupts
MASCAL as you demand to know if all's well.
BBC reports rockets slammed the Green Zone
near our hospital, multiple casualties. Thanks,
didn't know where this latest casualty batch
had come from.

Last time downrange, eavesdrop on soldiers'
sorrowful lament: daddy can't pick you up
buddy; mommy can't rock you to sleep.

Desperately trying to stay in touch with
distant loved ones back home, but cannot
touch what's virtually seen; there, but not
there, curse of the video chat app.

In future wars, distant lands, will loved
ones holographically patrol with grunts?
Going downrange no longer reason for
separation: chat, giggle, see we're okay.
'Til pink mist appears when distracted,
mistakenly dive on an exploding grenade
to protect who?

Five Years

Five years, doc kvetches in the upper Tigris
tent hospital, why's the system not primed,
greased, ready to go. It's difficult caring for
women deployed with abnormal smears, who
are told to follow up here. Send specimens,
but don't get results back. After five years,
you'd think the system would work.

Five years! Grievance heard over and again,
whenever someone gripes it doesn't work.

Been here five years but it takes forever to
transmit x-rays for interpretation, doc gripes.
Theater lacks bandwidth for swift relay; thus,
rad doc's diagnosis arrives too late to matter.
You'd think it would work after five years.

For five years, hospital CO complains,
prior COs worked to get drug analyzer;
treating drug overdoses a huge challenge.
Despite effort, don't expect analyzer soon.
Send out serum specimens and delayed
results are of no clinical consequence.

Most downrange healthcare works well:
fast med-evac, life-saving trauma care,
blood supply's a thing-of-beauty; all
refined through practice to perfection.
Even rape evals, regrettably, well-honed
from repeated reps. Saving grace all,

but still, most other inquiries launch
same story: here five-years and . . .

Weekend Warriors' Lament

That's the soccer field, reserve medic
says driving from air strip to hospital,
where, after a loss, Saddam shot his
soccer team. Says who? we ask.

Not missing a beat: our president!
That brings forth our mirth, you
believe what he says? Sure do,
as do you, or you'd not be here.

Pass through dreary, barren terrain:
you like deployment here? Which
draws an are-you-fricking-me glare.
Life's good, have all essentials:

place to work, place to eat,
place to shit, place to sleep.
Glad I came to this hellhole
for 12-month reserve tour,

double the time active-duty deploy.
Proud to serve the USA, do good for
worthy host nation. Surge working,
great progress, we're winning.

In the stifling OR, gas passer bitches
about his ancient, broken equipment. And
look at this grimy dust! Fingers sweep
OR table top; wiping away sweat he

smudges forehead in Lent like contrition.
AC, HEPA suck; surgeons, patients barely
survive surgery! But DFAC's clean, cold,
has an indirect-fire deflecting canopy.

Canvas covers us. Joined this reserve
hospital after 9/11; imagine ending up
here. Shakes head, no more elaboration.
Activated reserve nurse ponders the

coming end of her yearlong Iraq tour.
Worries what awaits on her return home.
Mortgage on the farmhouse is underwater;
dollar's now worth a dime; gas is up more

than two dollars a gallon. Can I even afford to
commute from home to my job nursing in our
community hospital? Do I still have a job?
Can't retire since 401(k) pension tanked

with the stock market. Finger combs hair,
lights cigarette. Could be worse; could be
going home maimed or in transfer carrier case
like so many who passed through my ward.

Broken Bike

Sandbox soldier bikes for exercise, has
a ten-click loop inside the perimeter wire.
Does four-laps daily, two-hours peddling.
Helps him stay in shape, alleviates stress.

First bike bought shortly after arrival;
tires soon shredded on shattered concrete.
Goes to the PX for tire-patch kit, bike
pump to fix the flats. PX sells neither;
only solution's to buy another bike.

He rotates soon, won't ship bikes home.
Leave 'em for next guy like all sporting
and electronics gear acquired when he
first moved into his CHU: stuff left
behind for next occupant to inherit.

Broken stuff everywhere in-country
abandoned by those here before.
Burned-out bulb lamps, dead-battery
alarm-clock radios, all the discarded
detritus that haunts every CHU.

Look around, lots of broken stuff here.
Filthy tap water, reeking toilets that don't
flush because pumps or pipes still busted,
never repaired. And no reliable electricity
to light the night, cool the day. Downed
wires, shattered generators all courtesy of
shock-and-awe invasion devastation.

Although plenty money, little has been
restored. Electricity, clean water, flushing
latrines, healthcare, all the necessities of
civilized life remains elusive, despite
years of occupation.

Return to Rules

Shouldn't be here without an escort!
MSG yells in men's latrine. If you insist,
ask her to step in, but she didn't show
any eagerness to accompany me.

Welcome to Kuwait. From the moment we
exit our C-17, face-to-face with haughty NCOs.
Off the bus from the flightline they shout:
line up with ID cards ready to scan.

Do this, do that; no "welcome back" from
downrange, grateful thanks, job well done.
As if regressed from soldiers to unruly recruits
the moment our boots hit Kuwaiti soil.

Rough greeting for soldiers after year in the
sandbox, shocking transition from the combat
zone. Ordered relinquish constant companion
mike-9 and round-laden magazines.

Glad to oblige since they never gave protective
comfort; mostly worries about their loss. Most
relieved when armory sarge declares mike-9
clean; daily baby-butt wipes did the trick.

Good riddance to bleached, delaminated,
subdued black-on-green flag; despite claim it
was night-scope visible, snipers said not so.
Replace with true red, white, and blue.

Kuwait's the mental airlock from downrange to
home, where off-duty civilian clothes wear okay,
but the radio's tuned to Baghdad AFN stations.
Like home but not yet home.

Parallel Universe in Arabia

Soldiers live in parallel universes in Arabia,
some on PCOS garrison-support assignments,
others deployed on hazardous-duty tours.
Different rules apply to each universe.

Garrison soldiers live off-post,
commute to-and-from work every day,
kids go to host nation schools,
spouses haggle at the local souk,
weapons strictly forbidden off-post.

Hazardous duty soldiers must carry
weapons off-post, follow strict ROE.
So when a soldier gets in a fender-bender
with a local, draws weapon during heated
argument over fault, fires shots in the air.

Gets in trouble not for weapon discharge;
for failure to use lethal force as required
by ROE. Should have killed the laborer,
not scare him. Makes no sense,
but there it is.

CID Takes Great Umbrage

CID agent at CIF perplexed: you
left your weapons in Islamabad?
We did indeed 'cause the
Gulf Air honcho wouldn't
clear our mike-9s for
the flight to Abu Dhabi.
So we handed 'em off to the
embassy military attaché.

This a malfeasance that
warrants great scrutiny, because
the loss of weapons a great
transgression, particularly
if relinquished weapons
should somehow turn
up in enemy hands.

We stress we had no desire
to be stranded in Islamabad,
due to lack of appropriate
paperwork from HQ. But agent
disparages our excuses, rejects our
wise command decision made
to ditch our weapons, rather
than place our lives in peril
overnighting in Pakistan.

Agent huffs this deliberate
sacrilegious surrender of
weapons in a hostile land,
a punishable UCMJ crime,
and is further alarmed by our
proposed counteroffer to write
checks covering the cost of
missing sidearms.

Rumor has it, but probably true,
issued gear carried downrange
is on loan from Uncle Sam.
Fail to return any and all items,
you'll pay the price, even if dead.
Well, then that burden falls
to your survivors.

Where's proof of your wild story?
If none, prepare for stockade time.
So hasty our departure, we barely
made the flight, didn't get receipts.
Perhaps contact the Islamabad
military attaché, get serial numbers
for our missing mike-9s.

And lo the story's confirmed,
now we're homeward bound,
wondering why soldiers merit
less value and concern than the
gear we carry.

Graffiti on the 332nd AFTH

Though now sun-bleached,
witness the departed healers'
words on the wall outside
the OR of the 332nd AFTH:

That A-line worked a minute ago!
Where's the blood?
Call the OR STAT!
Shutoff the medevac pipeline!
Living the dream.
I am THE black cloud.

And more spill over
onto the entryway:

Quit yelling at me!
I am not like this at home.
It's magic time.
I NEED coffee.
We're just playing.
What's up with this?
We're winning?!

And the casualties' echoes
are scrawled at the
evacuation transition point:

2 tours, 2 happy hospital visits.
Make that 3!!!
Heartfelt thanks for your care.
And too many KIA's names and dates.
You'll not be forgotten.
God bless America.

Alien words,
now rarely read
in a distant land.

Panel 23E

Among the 58,000 Vietnam fallen,
we find your name inscribed on
panel 23E of the black granite that
gashes into the sublime
National Mall:

near a nurse comforting a dying casualty
while her companion gazes forlornly skyward for
dust-off's arrival;

near three weary infantrymen returning from
outside the wire;

not far from, beyond the Great Emancipator,
19 silver-poncho'd Korean War combatants
who'll forever ghost along.

We recall that fateful day
you laid bare your soul over pitchers of beer:
failed the organic chem test,
childhood dream of healing now shattered,
dropping out,
giving up the quest
'cause you lack the grades
for med school entry.

No, we pleaded, your
fricking dropped-out
ass'll get drafted,
sent off to 'Nam!
You shrugged it off,

and by week’s end you’d gone.
Never to be heard from again
’til we see your name etched
on another monument of sacrifice
to feckless futility.

Lizard Brain

Lizard brain arrives on
the United triple 7 shuttle
from Kuwait to Dulles.
Attacks a dude in the

custom clearance line
who dared scoot around
luggage carts laden with
barrack bags filled with

war paraphernalia. We'd
lagged in line, wearily
opening a gap, so local
fast mover in suit pops

'round to fill the space.
Lizard brain grabs miscreant
by his suit lapels, lifts him
up onto his toes, until the

dude's grimace of terror
secures release. Sorry dude,
just back from serving
your ass in the sandbox.

Are you crazy or what?
Have PTSD or something?
Yeah, that's it: high octane
lizard brain.

Homecoming

It was a little-black thing
she wore,
and little more;

sparkling on ice
in a honking limousine,
joyous ride home to
the clamoring clan.

But soon the
choral ensemble discordant,
’cause bass doesn’t know the
newfangled rhythm or harmony

that alto, tenor, and soprano
of necessity in absence
had learned to master.

Borderland of Peace-Seeking

Fast-mover Blue Angels' roar
reverberates, resonates along
concrete canyons, glorifying
Fleet Week. Below,

peace clamoring agitators
crane necks to catch elusive
glimpses of warbirds rocketing
across the Frisco terrain.

We're war weary soldiers returned
from rendering downrange trauma
care, who seek succor and join the
peace-collaborators' march.

But their braying placards held high
declare ritual conspirator intrigue,
as they chant hey-hey, ho-ho,
bring the baby-killers home.

We find no solace here.
Disenthralled with fellow
travelers, we retreat to the
Ferry Terminal wine bar.

Who Them Guys

Much too late in dad’s life, we
ask which Field Artillery unit
yours on Anzio beach? Can’t
recall, he claimed. Heard Anzio
was a real meat grinder, any
details? Don’t recollect none.

When Uncle Clyde died, we
learned at his funeral about the
Silver Star and Purple Heart.
Don’t know when or where he
got ’em, something ’bout a battle
for a bulge. Uncle never said.

Uncle only talked about falling
asleep in a 6x6. He and the driver
awakened after slamming into a
huge oak tree; always astonished
’bout them acorns raining down.
Had nothing more to say.

Uncle Mark lost a leg in WWII.
Didn’t slow him down; drove
Caterpillars bulldozing Ike’s roads.
With Aunt Ruby raised ten kids in the
Catholic tradition and threat of a belt.
Mocked us for refusing to go to ’Nam.

Who them guys? Printer, farmer, heavy
equipment operator; family men, God-
fearing but not church goers. Never rich,
yet kept family clothed, fed, roof above.
Didn’t like us thinking Audie Murphy a
big deal, yet never shared what they saw.

Midlife, joined the Army, more for a job
than adventure. Of course, war came my
way; backfilled someone returning early.
A repo, said dad, over beers with Uncles
Mark and Clyde. Banal small talk, little
more. Grateful to join the soldiers' bond.

Wayward Veteran's Footstone

Dad's footstone's over his head!
What a screw up; how'd it happen?
You earned your veteran's footstone
on Anzio Beachhead.

Yeah, WWII blindsided you. After the
Day of Infamy shock, you reluctantly
volunteered, didn't wait to be drafted
or hide out in the National Guard.

Field Artillery radio operator trained to
direct 155 Long Tom rifle fire; sent ashore
on Anzio Beach with just enough to secure
a beachhead, not enough to move inland.

Spoke of a buddy blown to kingdom come by
enemy-artillery fire that reached everywhere
on the beach. After breakout, fought up Italian
Peninsula to France. Little said about that: only

something about a young woman willing,
too bad you had a wife, son back home
waiting. Rotated stateside for chemical
artillery training; yeah, Japan invasion

expected to be that bad. Instead, after
two devastating atomic blasts, came
home to farm, growing family, march
in Veteran's Day parades. Now an errant

veteran's footstone after meeting life's
fickle trajectory with few complaints?!
Your veteran's funeral a real tear-jerker.
Color guard, spiffy in scarlet-and-blue

Marine-dress uniforms, a great sendoff;
you'd've stood tall during the rifle salute.
But the footstone placed over your head,
screwed it up. Big concrete chunk, really

augured in. Move it? They laugh; cheaper
to disinter and re-bury you six feet farther
south. So, dad, we don't know what to do.
What say you, dad, you get a vote.

Yeah, we see your slight shake of head, a
little chuckle as you gaze at fellow dogface
soldiers up there and say: just another snafu
in a fubar world.

Veteran's Day

Stick walking the beach,
pedometer click clacks
the metrics of the trek.
Lost your skis, sir? The
passing jester quips.

Glistening lines overhead
entice elusive ocean prey,
while shrieking tots turn
away as they embrace
the saline smash.

Poling down the sand,
through the ivory froth,
where stealthy threads
of orbs' blue-stained fire
streak the lonely sole.

Retrace lopsided track as
dog gaggles frolic after ball
and disc. Inquisitive brindle
menaces sinister-alien limb,
retreats to master's plea.

Weary now head home under
sprawling Kalama Hau to rest.
Wrapped in musty poncho liners
on trash bags full of regret, an
old soldier's fateful sleep.

About the Author

James Allen Breitweser is a retired US Army Medical Corps Officer who has had combat zone tours. He earned an MD in Medicine from the University of Minnesota as well as an MA in Communication from Hawaii Pacific University. His poems have been published in *As You Were* (Military Experience and the Arts) and the *Veterans' Voices* (Veterans Voices Writing Project). He lives with his wife in Hawaii.

www.ingramcontent.com/pod-product-compliance
Lightning Source LLC
LaVergne TN
LVHW010630100826
845148LV00014B/3184
9781639803859